MW01644421
Butterflies
Rainbows
& Flowers

HELLO *and* WELCOME *to*

Butterflies, Rainbows & Flowers

by Blue Jewel Books

HAVE A SUPER FUN TIME!

We create our books with great love and care yet mistakes beyond our control can happen in printing, binding and shipping. If you have any questions, comments, concerns, or problems with this book please contact us at: bluejewelbooks@gmail.com.

Published by Blue Jewel Books

Spread
your
Wings
and
Fly

Love
Butterflies

I AM
Beautiful

YOU ARE A

Rainbow

OF POSSIBILITIES

RAINBOWS
Make Me
Happy

Be Happy

I Believe
I can fly

TRY OUT A BONUS COLORING PAGE FROM OUR BOOK: SUPER CUTE COLORING

TRY OUT A BONUS COLORING PAGE FROM OUR BOOK: CUTE MANDALAS